Where did the Statue of Liberty come from?

Disney *BOOKS BY MAIL*

DK Direct Limited
Managing Art Editor Eljay Crompton
Senior Editor Rosemary McCormick
Writer Alexandra Parsons
Illustrators The Alvin White Studios and Richard Manning
Designers Wayne Blades, Veneta Bullen, Richard Clemson,
Sarah Goodwin, Diane Klein, Sonia Whillock , Richard Starzecki

Contents

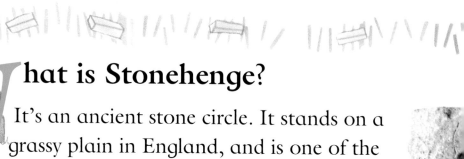

What is Stonehenge?

It's an ancient stone circle. It stands on a grassy plain in England, and is one of the most mysterious structures on Earth. Some people think that Stonehenge was built about 4,000 years ago and was used as a religious center and meeting place. Others think that it may have been used by wise men to study the sun and the moon. But no one really knows why it was built – or when.

4

Old stone facts

Stonehenge used to have more stones than it does now. But, over the years, some of them have fallen down. Others were taken away to make bridges and dams.

Long ago, people believed that Stonehenge was brought to England by a magician called Merlin.

Heave ho!
The people who built
Stonehenge didn't have
any machinery. They
probably used wooden
poles and ropes to pull
each stone into place.

Heavy work
Building Stonehenge must have been
hard work. Some of the stones
weighed as much as 60 men.

Where can you find a lost city?

In the mountains of Peru is the city of Machu Picchu (MA-choo PE-choo). It was built by the Incas, who once ruled much of South America. But, when their lands were captured, Machu Picchu was deserted. Over time, weeds covered the crumbling city and hid it from view. Nearly 400 years went by before it was found again – by an explorer in search of another lost city.

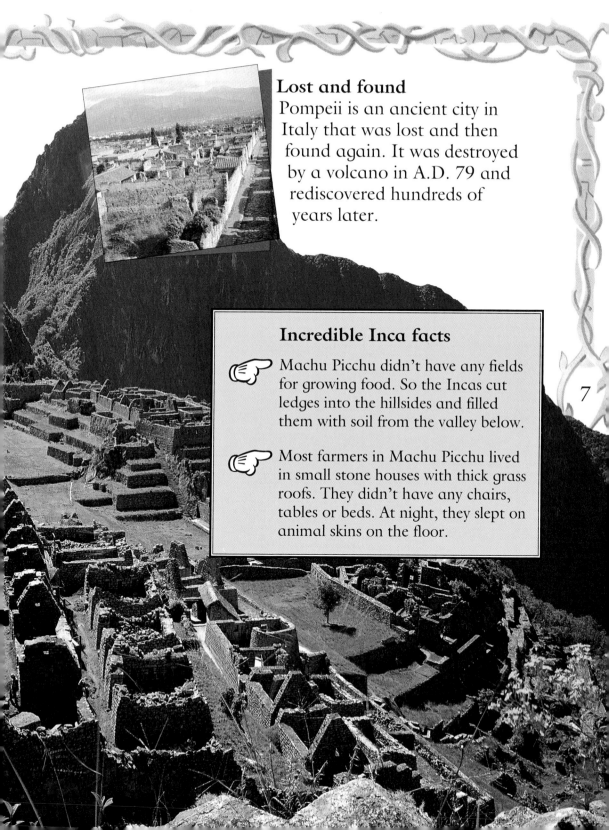

Lost and found

Pompeii is an ancient city in Italy that was lost and then found again. It was destroyed by a volcano in A.D. 79 and rediscovered hundreds of years later.

Incredible Inca facts

Machu Picchu didn't have any fields for growing food. So the Incas cut ledges into the hillsides and filled them with soil from the valley below.

Most farmers in Machu Picchu lived in small stone houses with thick grass roofs. They didn't have any chairs, tables or beds. At night, they slept on animal skins on the floor.

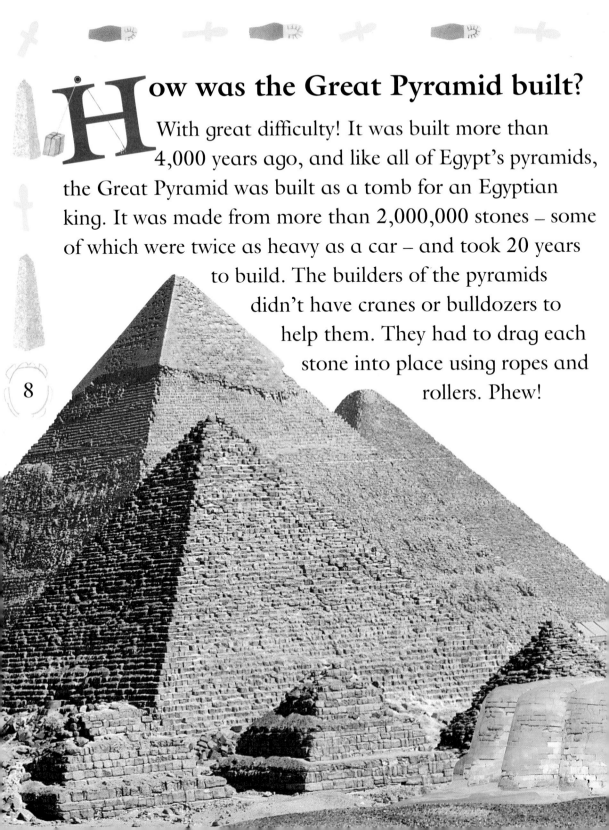

How was the Great Pyramid built?

With great difficulty! It was built more than 4,000 years ago, and like all of Egypt's pyramids, the Great Pyramid was built as a tomb for an Egyptian king. It was made from more than 2,000,000 stones – some of which were twice as heavy as a car – and took 20 years to build. The builders of the pyramids didn't have cranes or bulldozers to help them. They had to drag each stone into place using ropes and rollers. Phew!

Colorful coffins
Rich Egyptians were often buried in highly decorated coffins.

The inside story
 The ancient Egyptians believed that a dead person needed the same things as a living person. So they packed the tombs inside the pyramids with food, furniture, treats, and treasures.

Pyramid puzzle
Why didn't the Egyptians build their pyramids in the fog? **They couldn't see the point!**

Rock watch
This stone statue is called the Sphinx. It has guarded Egypt's most famous pyramids for thousands of years.

Who built the Great Wall of China?

The Chinese! The Great Wall of China is the longest wall in the world. In fact, it's so long it can be seen from the moon. Chinese workers started building this wall more than 2,000 years ago. They hoped that it would keep their enemies out.

Dragon tales
The Great Wall twists across China like a giant, swirly dragon. Storytellers say that this is because a helpful dragon marked out the path of the wall for the workers.

Fruity fun
What's purple and thousands of miles long?
The Grape Wall of China!

Great Wall facts

☞ All along the wall, there are lots of watchtowers.

☞ If the wall was attacked, guards inside the watchtowers lit fires to warn soldiers far away.

☞ The Chinese built a wide road along the top of the wall. This made it easier for soldiers to reach each watchtower quickly.

Which building looks good enough to eat?

Saint Basil's cathedral in Moscow, Russia. Its nine curved roofs, called domes, are so colorful they look like candy drops or even ice cream cones. Saint Basil's isn't just one church, though. It's really eight small churches bunched around a larger one. It was built about 450 years ago by a mean and moody Russian ruler named Ivan the Terrible.

Snow slide
Lots of churches in Russia have domes shaped like onions. This shape helps stop snow from piling up on the roof.

13

Church chat

☞ Ivan the Terrible's cathedral is called Saint Basil's because Ivan's favorite helper, Basil, is buried inside it.

☞ Many cathedrals have tall, pointed towers on their roofs to encourage people to look up to heaven.

Is the Tower of Pisa supposed to lean?

NO! The Tower of Pisa in Italy is supposed to be straight. But soon after work on it began, the soil underneath it sank and it started to tilt. The tower is about 700 years old – and tilting more than ever. If it keeps on leaning more each year, it will soon topple over!

Look out!
Hundreds of years ago, wealthy Italians sometimes built towers on their palaces. They used these towers to keep a look out for enemies – and to show off to their friends.

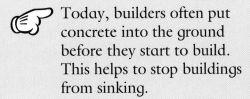

Hard facts

👉 Today, builders often put concrete into the ground before they start to build. This helps to stop buildings from sinking.

👉 Much of the Tower of Pisa is made from a rock called marble.

👉 Once upon a time, visitors were allowed to climb to the top of the Tower of Pisa. But they're not allowed to anymore because it's too risky.

15

Comic cookies
What did the cookie say
when it fell off the
Tower of Pisa?
Oh, crumbs!

What's so special about the Taj Mahal?

The Taj Mahal in India is one of the most beautiful buildings in the world. It was built more than 300 years ago as a tomb for an Indian empress. It is made of creamy marble, which seems to change color during the day. At sunrise it looks pink. At midday, it looks brilliant white. And at nighttime it looks a ghostly gray.

Amazing mosques
Many mosques have elegant decorations too. Mosques are holy places of a religion called Islam.

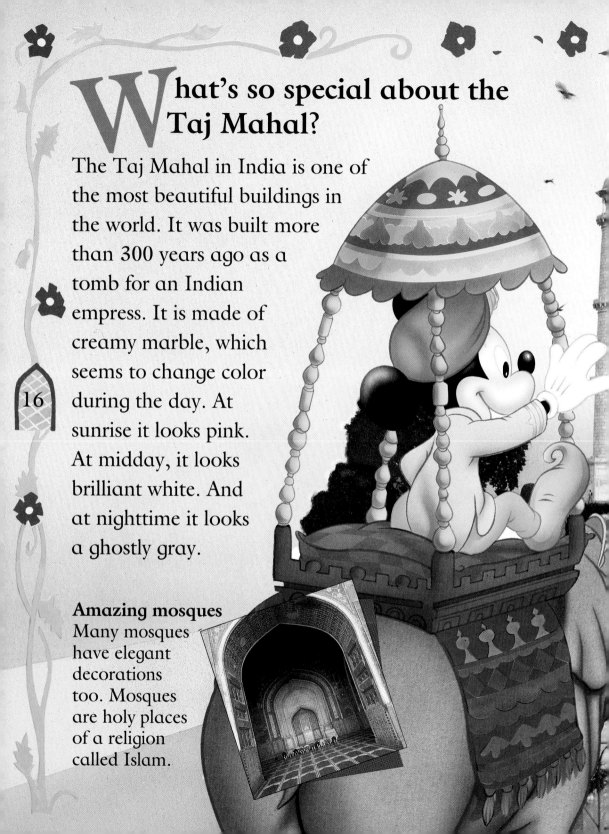

Taj talk

The Taj Mahal stands in a peaceful walled garden.

It took 20,000 men about 20 years to build the Taj Mahal.

The empress buried in the Taj was named Mumtaz Mahal. When she died, her husband showered her coffin with diamonds and pearls.

How many rooms are in Buckingham Palace?

About 600. That includes 240 bedrooms, 92 offices and 78 toilets and bathrooms. No wonder lots of people are needed to keep the building neat and tidy. Today, part of the palace is used as a work place and museum. The rest is used by the Queen and her family, whenever they're in London.

Anyone home?
If a flag is flying from the roof of Buckingham Palace, you know that the Queen is at home.

Cleaning-up

☞ The royal banquet table in Buckingham Palace is SO large, that to keep it gleaming, a member of staff has to tie dusters to his feet and polish it as he slides across it!

All change!
The changing-of-the-guard ceremony at Buckingham Palace is a popular sight. Guards in bearskin hats march in front of the palace. Then they swap places with those who have already been on duty.

How tall is the Eiffel Tower?

It's 1,010 feet tall. That's about the same size as 100 elephants standing on each other's shoulders. Like most tall, thin buildings, the Eiffel Tower sways in strong winds. But it doesn't snap. This is because its frame – which is made of iron – is strengthened by criss-crossed pieces which help support the structure. Inside the tower, there's a staircase so people can reach the top.

Strange but true facts

A man once rode up the Eiffel Tower on a horse.

Someone rode all the way down the tower on a bicycle.

And believe it or not, one man took an elephant up the tower with him.

Jumping joke!
Can Mickey jump higher
than the Eiffel Tower?
**Sure! The Eiffel Tower
can't jump!**

**Merry Christmas,
Paris**
The Eiffel Tower is
in Paris, France. At
Christmas it is lighted
up to wish all of Paris
a happy holiday.

21

Where did the Statue of Liberty come from?

It came from France. It was given to the people of the United States by the people of France as a sign of their friendship. The statue was built in Paris and sent to New York by ship. But it wasn't gift wrapped and sent in one piece. It is far too big for that. Instead, it was taken apart, packed in boxes, and put together again in New York.

Up on top
There is a stairway inside Miss Liberty which winds up to her crown. From there visitors get a good view of New York City and the harbor. And they can wave to their pals below!

Night Lights

The statue's torch flame is covered with gold. At night, lamps in the torch rim shine on the flame and make it glow.

Liberty facts and figures

☞ The Statue of Liberty is HUGE. Her nose alone is four-and-a-half feet long.

☞ Liberty has a metal frame underneath her copper "skin." This frame stops her from breaking in fierce winds.

☞ In 1986, New York threw a BIG party to celebrate Miss Liberty's 100th birthday.

S S

What is carved on the side of Mount Rushmore?

The heads of four great American presidents. The workers who made these heads blasted the mountain rock with dynamite, and carved the faces with drills. They used small models of the presidents to guide them as they worked. All four heads took 14 years to complete. They are now one of America's famous tourist sights.

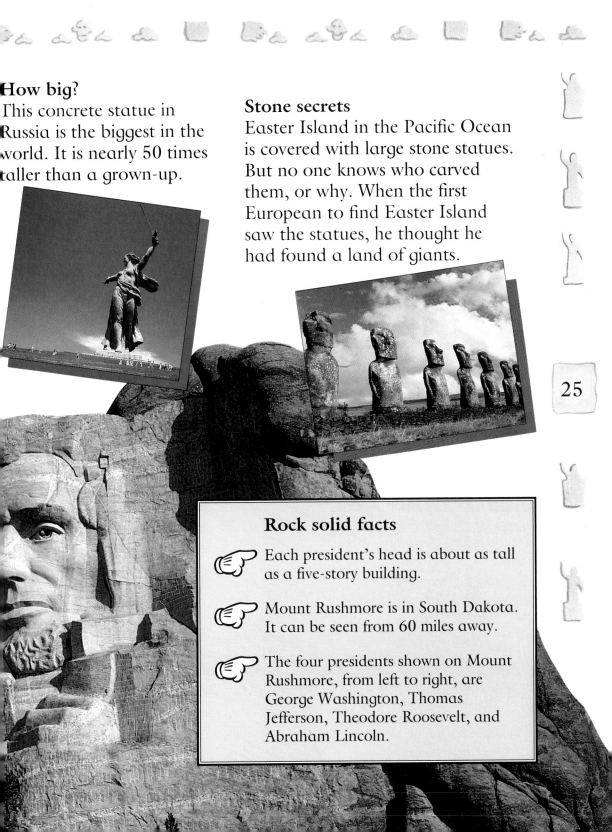

How big?
This concrete statue in Russia is the biggest in the world. It is nearly 50 times taller than a grown-up.

Stone secrets
Easter Island in the Pacific Ocean is covered with large stone statues. But no one knows who carved them, or why. When the first European to find Easter Island saw the statues, he thought he had found a land of giants.

Rock solid facts

☞ Each president's head is about as tall as a five-story building.

☞ Mount Rushmore is in South Dakota. It can be seen from 60 miles away.

☞ The four presidents shown on Mount Rushmore, from left to right, are George Washington, Thomas Jefferson, Theodore Roosevelt, and Abraham Lincoln.

Which sports stadium looks like a giant tent?

The Olympic stadium in Munich, Germany. Its roof is made from metal netting covered with clear plastic. It hangs down from huge metal posts, and is held at the edges by strong wires. The smart thing about this roof is that it lets in light, but not rain. Also, because its supporting posts are outside the stadium, no one's view is blocked.

26

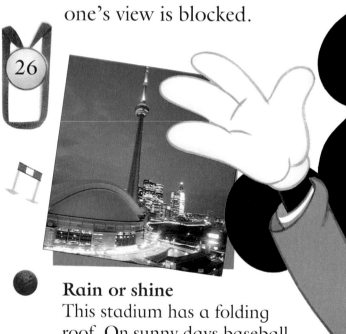

Rain or shine

This stadium has a folding roof. On sunny days baseball games are played with the roof open. And on rainy days they are played with the roof shut.

Wacky stadium facts

Some sports stadiums have strange and wonderful shapes. There's a sports stadium shaped like a saddle, there's one shaped like a bent hoola-hoop, and there's even one shaped like an oyster shell.

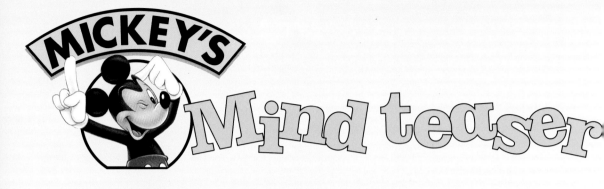

Can you remember where these famous monuments can be found?